CHUPACABRAS

PETER CASTELLANO

HOT
TOPICS

 Gareth Stevens
PUBLISHING

Please visit our website, www.garethstevens.com. For a free color catalog of all our high-quality books, call toll free 1-800-542-2595 or fax 1-877-542-2596.

Library of Congress Cataloging-in-Publication Data

Castellano, Peter, author.
 Chupacabras / Peter Castellano.
    pages cm. — (Monsters!)
 Includes bibliographical references and index.
 ISBN 978-1-4824-4082-9 (pbk.)
 ISBN 978-1-4824-4083-6 (6 pack)
 ISBN 978-1-4824-4084-3 (library binding)
 1. Chupacabras—Juvenile literature. I. Title.
 QL89.2.C57C37 2016
 001.944—dc23
                            2015021472

First Edition

Published in 2016 by
Gareth Stevens Publishing
111 East 14th Street, Suite 349
New York, NY 10003

Designer: Samantha DeMartin
Editor: Kristen Nelson

Photo credits: Cover, pp. 1, 29 Alexlky/Shutterstock.com; pp. 5, 21, 23 courtesy of Benjamin Radford; p. 7 © iStockphoto.com/raddanovic; p. 9 (paper) © iStockphoto.com/Eivaisla; p. 9 (drawing) LeCire/Wikimedia Commons; p. 11 Michael Lynch/Shutterstock.com; p. 13 courtesy of Derek Edgerton; p. 15 Matt Knoth/Shutterstock.com; pp. 17, 27 Eric Gay/ AP Images; p. 19 Zeng Chanwen/ICHPL Imaginechina/AP Images; p. 25 Suphatthra China/Shutterstock.com; p. 30 Paul Stringer/Shutterstock.com.

Printed in the United States of America

CPSIA compliance information: Batch #CW16GS: For further information contact Gareth Stevens, New York, New York at 1-800-542-2595.

CONTENTS

SPOTTED!

In 1995, a Puerto Rican woman named Madelyne Tolentino reported seeing a truly scary **creature** outside her home near the city of San Juan. She only saw it for a couple minutes, but those minutes started a **legend**—the chupacabra!

BEYOND THE MYTH

The chupacabra is a common subject of cryptozoologists. Cryptozoology is the study of animals that may or may not be real.

ANIMAL KILLER

At the time, people nearby were finding their farm animals dead. No explanation had been found. Tolentino told Puerto Rican newspapers about what she saw. People began to believe they'd figured out what killed the animals!

BEYOND THE MYTH

Some people say the story of the chupacabra dates back to the 1960s or 1970s. However, Tolentino's sighting appears to be the first.

Tolentino said the creature she saw was about 4 feet (1.2 m) tall and stood on two legs. She said it had dark eyes, thin arms, and three fingers on each hand. After Tolentino's story was on the news, more people reported seeing the chupacabra!

BEYOND THE MYTH

There weren't any photographs taken or footprints found from these early chupacabra sightings.

VAMPIRE

"Chupacabra" means "goat sucker." It's believed to be an animal that kills farm animals and sucks out all their blood! Since other animals are known **vampires**, such as the vampire bat, why couldn't the chupacabra be one?

BEYOND THE MYTH

The claim that the animals were drained, or emptied, of blood has since been found to be untrue. When **examined**, animals supposedly killed by a chupacabra still had lots of blood in them.

NEWS SPREADS FAST

Once it hit the Internet, the story of the chupacabra quickly spread beyond Puerto Rico. Chupacabra sightings began occurring in Mexico, Chile, Nicaragua, and even Florida! The **descriptions** people gave of the creature sounded a lot like Tolentino's.

BEYOND THE MYTH

TV news shows and newspapers gave a very clear description of Tolentino's chupacabra. That's likely why the other chupacabra sightings were the same as hers.

WHAT DOES IT LOOK LIKE?

Around the year 2000, sightings of the chupacabra began to change. First of all, gone was the two-legged creature. People began saying the chupacabra had four legs and looked somewhat like a hairless dog or coyote.

BEYOND THE MYTH

Canines, or animals in the dog family, couldn't be draining animals of blood. Their mouths can't create the seal needed to suck blood like a vampire would.

The other change was where the sightings were occurring. By around 2005, many chupacabra sightings were happening in Texas and the southwestern United States. Bodies of supposed chupacabras began to be examined. People wanted to know if the creatures were real!

BEYOND THE MYTH

Even today, chupacabra sightings happen in places where many people speak Spanish, owing to the legend's roots in Latin America.

07/14/2007

17

SPACE CREATURE

The chupacabra's origins, or beginnings, have been talked about almost as much as sightings of the creature. Some say the chupacabra came from space. Others believe the National Aeronautics and Space Administration (NASA) created it by accident!

BEYOND THE MYTH

The chupacabra has been said to be the source of AIDS, a terrible illness scientists know came to humans from chimpanzees in west Africa.

19

CHUPACABRA SPECIALIST

Much of what we now know about the history of the chupacabra comes from 5 years of work done by Benjamin Radford. His book, *Tracking the Chupacabra: The Vampire Beast in Fact, Fiction, and Folklore,* came out in 2011.

BEYOND THE MYTH

Radford said the spit of a vampire animal would have an anticoagulant, or matter that doesn't allow bleeding to stop. No animals said to be chupacabras have had this.

Radford is the one who tracked down Tolentino's report as the first sighting of the chupacabra. While talking to her, Radford found out she'd just seen a movie called *Species*—and her description of the chupacabra matched that of the alien in that movie.

BEYOND THE MYTH

After discovering this, Radford said, "It's not unfair to say that Hollywood created the chupacabra in a very real way."

MADELYNE TOLENTINO

23

MANGE

As for the doglike chupacabras sighted in United States, there seems to be an explanation for them, too! Scientists and vets have been able to examine some of the "chupacabras." Many are coyotes, wolves, and raccoons sick with an illness called mange.

BEYOND THE MYTH

Tiny bugs called mites cause mange. It makes animals' skin get thicker, and they lose their hair. Sometimes mangy animals smell. They're weakened, too, which may be why they go after farm animals rather than faster food.

25

Even with all the **evidence** against the chupacabra, people *still* report sightings! In 2014, a couple in Ratcliffe, Texas, caught an animal they thought was a baby chupacabra. They fed it cat food and corn!

BEYOND THE MYTH

Soon after stories about the Ratcliffe chupacabra were all over the news, the animal was found to be a raccoon with mange.

27

KEEP LOOKING?

It's fun to believe in legends like the chupacabra! It also makes a great news story. What do you think? Should scientists still be on the lookout for this dangerous creature?

BEYOND THE MYTH

When you hear or read a story that isn't backed up by evidence, consider who is reporting it. Knowing how to judge a **source** well is an important skill!

29

Spotting the Chupacabra

ALBUQUERQUE, NM
2007

RATCLIFFE, TX
2014

JALISCO, MEXICO
1995

SAN JUAN, PUERTO RICO
1995

MALPAISILLO, NICARAGUA
2000

Check out some of the places people have reported seeing chupacabras. Where will this monster be spotted next?

BOOKS

Anderson, Holly Lynn. *Unexplained Monsters and Cryptids.* Pittsburgh, PA: Eldorado Ink, 2015.

Roberts, Steven. *Chupacabras.* New York, NY: PowerKids Press, 2013.

WEBSITES

Central American Folklore

americanfolklore.net/folklore/2010/07/central_american_folklore.html

Find out about more myths and legends of Latin America.

Chupacabra Facts

channel.nationalgeographic.com/wild/the-monster-project/articles/chupacabra-facts/

Read some more fun facts about el chupacabra!

description: words that tell how something looks and sounds

evidence: something that helps show or disprove the truth of something

examine: to look something over carefully

legend: a story that has been passed down for many, many years that's unlikely to be true

source: a supplier of knowledge, factual or otherwise

vampire: a made-up being who drinks human blood